LISA WHEELER

MAMMOTHS
ON THE
MOVE

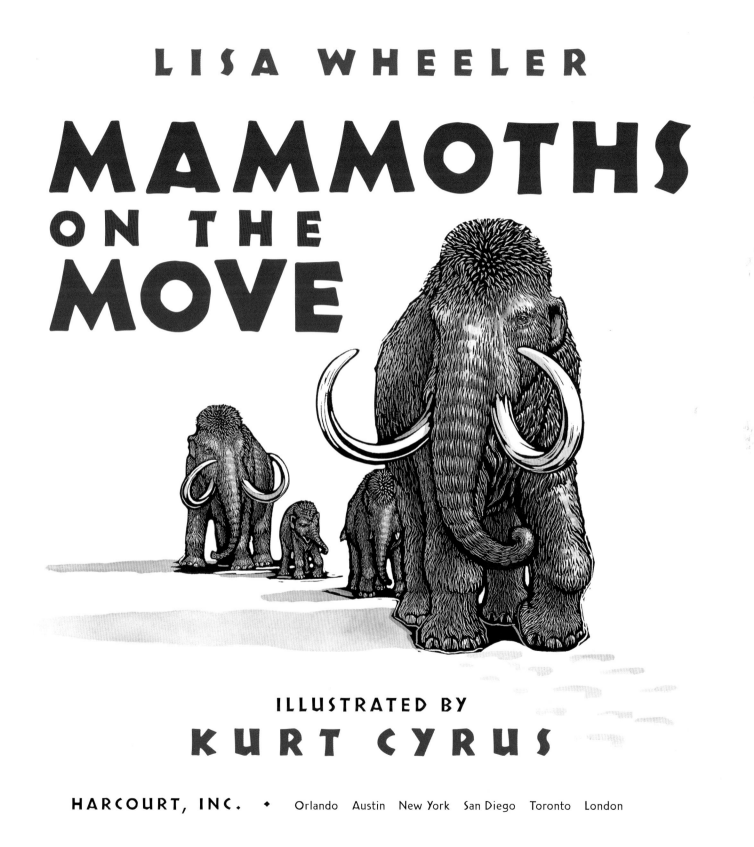

ILLUSTRATED BY
KURT CYRUS

HARCOURT, INC. ◆ Orlando Austin New York San Diego Toronto London

A Note from the Author

Because mammoths have been extinct for thousands of years, very little is known about them. We do know that during the Ice Age vast plains called the mammoth steppes extended from Northern Europe, across Asia, and into North America. And we know that during the time period in which this story takes place, North America was home to three kinds of mammoths: the woolly mammoth, the Columbian mammoth, and the Jefferson mammoth.

The habits and behaviors of the mammoths in this book are based on the latest scientific research. But in some cases, the only clue as to what mammoths did or how they behaved is their surviving kin, the elephant. For instance, by observing how elephants swim across large bodies of water, we can guess that their cousins, the mammoths, swam in much the same way.

Whatever the specifics of mammoth behavior, we can be certain of one thing: These mighty, majestic creatures will forever provoke curiosity and inspire awe in humankind.

Requests for permission to make copies of any part of the work should be mailed to the following address: Permissions Department, Harcourt, Inc., 6277 Sea Harbor Drive, Orlando, Florida 32887-6777.

www.HarcourtBooks.com

Library of Congress Cataloging-in-Publication Data
Wheeler, Lisa, 1963–
Mammoths on the move/Lisa Wheeler; illustrated by Kurt Cyrus.
p. cm.
1. Woolly mammoth—Juvenile literature. I. Cyrus, Kurt, ill. II. Title.
QE882.P8W48 2006
569'.67—dc22 2004019112
ISBN-13: 978-0152-04700-9 ISBN-10: 0-15-204700-X

The illustrations in this book were done in scratchboard and watercolor.
The display type was set in Neueneuland Solid.
The text type was set in Neueneuland Light.
Color separations by Colourscan Co. Pte. Ltd., Singapore
Manufactured by South China Printing Company, Ltd., China
This book was printed on totally chlorine-free Stora Enso Matte paper.
Production supervision by Ginger Boyer
Designed by Linda Lockowitz

First edition
H G F E D C B A

Manufactured in China

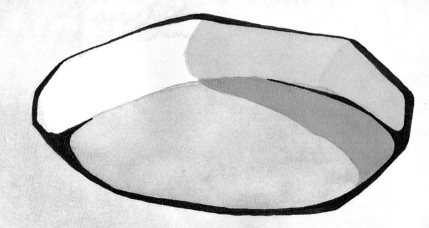

Mammoth thanks to the librarians, clerks,
and pages at the Trenton Veterans Memorial Library
for all their help and support.
Also, a gigantic hug for Snuffy, my first love.
—L. W.

Fourteen thousand years ago
the north was mostly ice and snow.
But woolly mammoths didn't care—
these beasts had comfy coats of hair.

Fuzzy, shaggy,
snarly, snaggy,
**wonderful
woolly mammoths!**

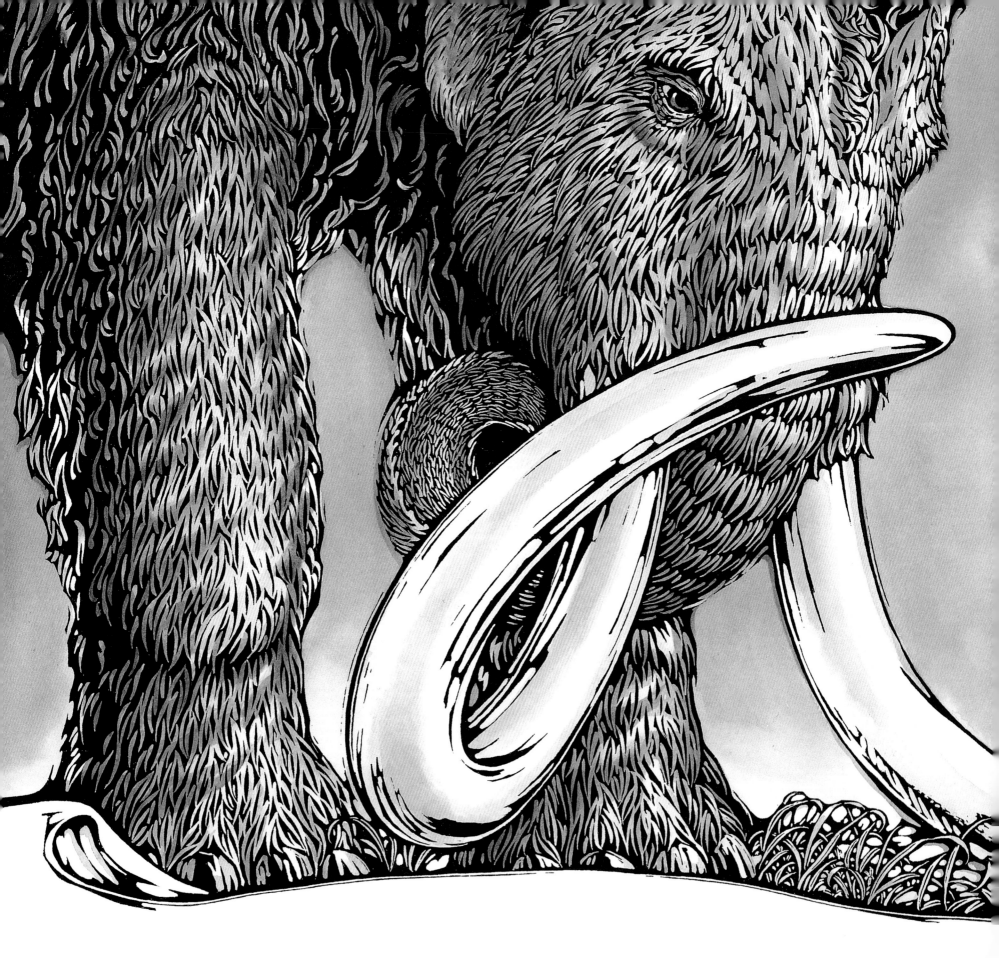

They grazed on grass and arctic moss
that grew above the permafrost.
In family herds, they liked to dine
on tender herbs of summertime.

Two toothy tusks grew down and out
and as they swung their heads about,
they swept the tundra clear of snow
to reach the shoots concealed below.

Grinding, gnawing,
chewing, chawing,
wise and woolly mammoths!

Come colder days, those mammoth herds
migrated south, just like the birds.
Their menu had to be improved,
so mammoths packed their trunks and moved.

Their feet like snowshoes, wide and flat,
had rough-skinned soles designed so that
they would not slip on ice and snow.
Steady mammoths—time to go!

Stepping, stomping,
marching, tromping—
**Watch out,
woolly mammoths!**

The oldest mother led the way
across the steppes both night and day.
The females followed in her tracks,
majestic glaciers at their backs.

Rivers ran across their path
but mammoths didn't mind a bath.
They raised their snorkel-trunks up high
and swam with noses to the sky.

Swimming, pacing,
never racing—
This way,
woolly mammoths!

The mammoths' route was fraught with danger—
melting ice, a hunting stranger.
Woolly calves soon learned to fear
a saber-tooth, a human's spear.

Each mammoth had to guard her child,
for carnivores both fierce and wild
would prey upon the small or frail,
attacking travelers on the trail.

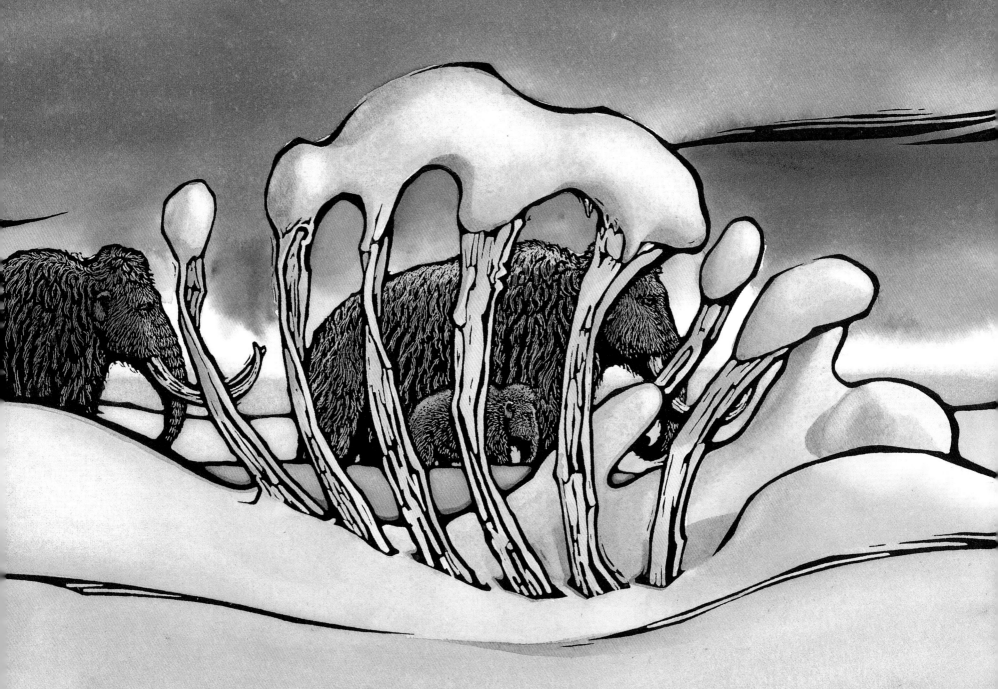

Tramping, lumbering,
trembling, thundering,
wary woolly mammoths!

If predators came moving in,
the cautious mammoth warned her kin
by trumpeting a warning call:
Danger! Danger! Danger, all!

When mothers heard that blaring sound
they formed a giant fortress round
their little calves to keep them snug
and safe within a woolly hug.

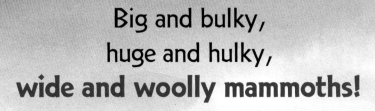

Big and bulky,
huge and hulky,
wide and woolly mammoths!

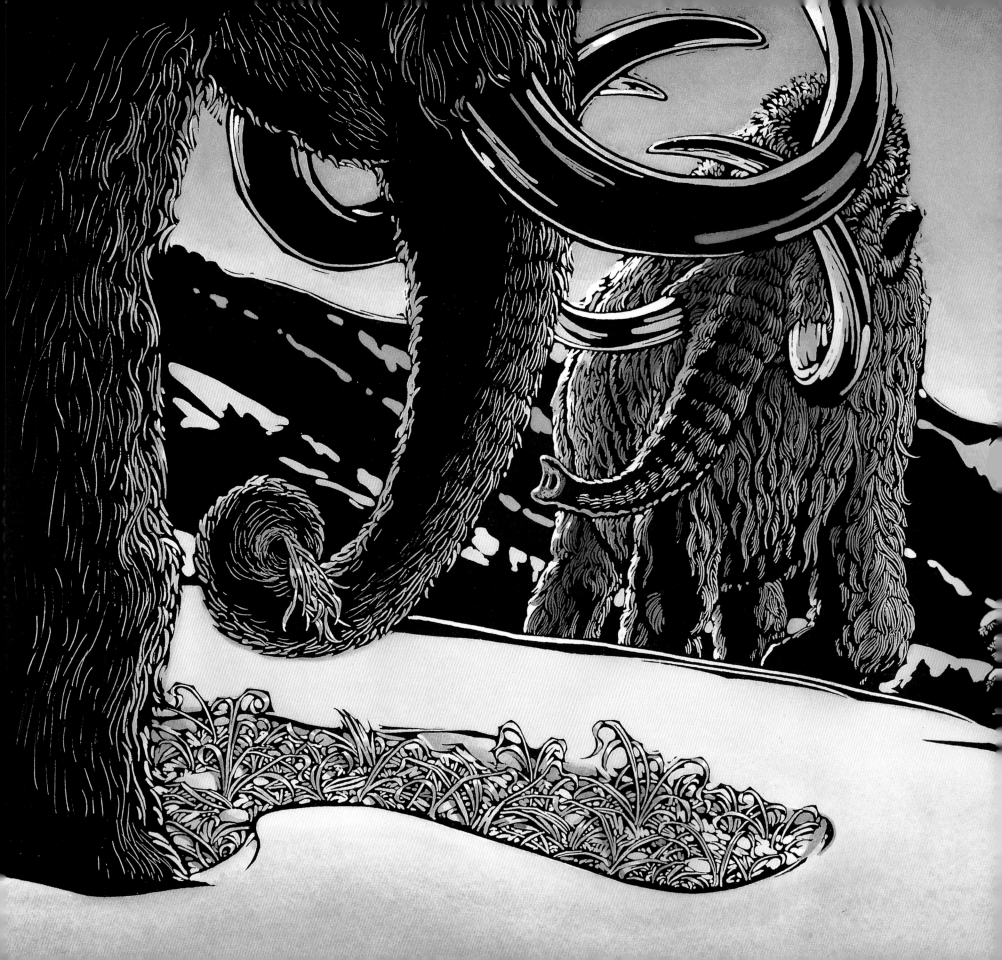

Each mammoth male was called a bull.
They liked to keep their tummies full.
Bulls ate and ate from morn till night.
They had a *mammoth* appetite.

Far from the herd, the bulls kept pace.
This gave the moms some breathing space
from males who liked to strut their stuff
to see which one was tough enough.

Sparring, crashing,
butting, clashing,
wild and woolly mammoths!

The calves, like children, joined in play.
Their moms made sure they wouldn't stray.
The trek was long, but you can bet
no mammoth whined . . .

"Are we there yet?"

Through storms that raged, through blinding snow,
the herd moved on, their pace was slow.
By instinct pulled . . . by hunger drawn,
they traveled on . . . and on . . . and on.

Plodding, trekking,
trudging, treading,
willful woolly mammoths!

Week by week and day by day
the mammoth family made its way.
They reached the south by winter's end . . .

. . . then started heading north again!

Massive, hairy,
legendary,
wonderful woolly mammoths!